Christmas Programs
for Children

Compiled by
Elaina Meyers

Plays, poems, and ideas for a joyful celebration!

Standard
PUBLISHING
Bringing The Word to Life

www.standardpub.com

Scripture taken from the HOLY BIBLE, NEW INTERNATIONAL VERSION®. NIV®. Copyright © 1973, 1978, 1984 by Biblica, Inc™. Used by permission of Zondervan. All rights reserved.

Scripture quotations marked (KJV) are taken from the King James Version.

Editorial team: Elaina Meyers, Courtney Rice
Cover design: Brigid Naglich
Inside design: Bob Korth

Published by Standard Publishing, Cincinnati, Ohio
www.standardpub.com
Copyright © 2010 by Standard Publishing
All rights reserved.

ISBN 978-0-7847-2354-8

Contents

DRAMAS & SKITS

Toys to the World 5
Dixie Phillips
Children learn that it's more blessed to give than to receive.

Were You There? 8
Carol S. Redd
An attempt to interview some of those who were there
when Jesus was born.

A Life Changing Experience 12
Marsha R. Chudy
The members of the youth group are asked to take part in
the Living Nativity play. Much to their surprise, it turns out
to be a life changing experience for them.

Come to My Party 18
Iris Gray Dowling
Mike, disappointed when no one came to his first party,
prepares a new invitation to a Christmas/birthday party
to tell why Jesus came from Heaven.

Frankenstein and Myrrh 22
John Cosper
Children practicing a Christmas drama learn about the
gifts that baby Jesus received and what the gifts stood for.

The Toys Nobody Wants 25
John Cosper
Department store toys, left on the shelves on
Christmas Eve, discuss the true meaning of Christmas.

The Great Debate **29**
Dianne McIntosh
Two teams debate the real reason for Christmas.

The Star **36**
Lenora McWhorter

POEMS **37**

Toys to the World

DIXIE PHILLIPS

Summary: Children learn that it's more blessed to give than to receive.
Characters: ZEKE, TUCKER
Setting: Two friends playing in a park one afternoon.
Props: park bench, baseball cap, book, toy truck with price tag showing, toy helicopter with price tag showing
Running Time: 13 minutes

ZEKE: *[wearing a baseball cap, holding his toy truck and helicopter above his head, and singing loudly]* Toys to the world, the Lord has some! *[sung to the tune of "Joy to the World"]*

TUCKER: *[sitting on park bench, reading a book; after hearing Zeke looks up with puzzled look on his face]* Zeke, what are you singing?

ZEKE: Hi, Tucker! I'm singing my favorite Christmas song of all time. *[sings it again louder]* Toys to the world, the Lord has some!

TUCKER: Don't you mean *[sings]* Joy to the world, the Lord has come?

ZEKE: I like it singing it this way. *[sings it again louder]* Toys to the world, the Lord has some!

TUCKER: Zeke, you can't sing, "Toys to the world, the Lord has some!" The right words are "Joy to the world, the Lord has come."

ZEKE: *[shakes head]* Picky! Picky! Picky! *[sings]* Toys to the world, the Lord has some!

TUCKER: I'm really not trying to be picky, Zeke. I just happen to know the right words because in the children's Christmas play I am singing the first verse of "Joy to the World." These are the words, Zeke. Now listen . . . *[clears throat and sings]* Joy to the world, the Lord is come.

ZEKE: *[listens intently and nods his head]* You have a nice voice, Tucker, but I like my version better. *[sings]* Toys to the world, the Lord has some!

TUCKER: *[slaps his forehead]* Zeke, our Sunday school teacher taught us that Christmas isn't about us getting lots and lots of toys. We celebrate it because of Jesus' birthday.

ZEKE: I know that, Tucker. That's what I am doing—celebrating Jesus' birthday. *[sings]* Toys to the world, the Lord has some!

TUCKER: *[holds his breath and turns red]* And the minister said that Christmas isn't about getting but about giving. Remember our memory verse? *[quoting]* It's more blessed to give than to receive.

ZEKE: Tucker, I know that. Our families sit together at church. I hear the same Bible stories that you do.

TUCKER: *[shakes finger in his friend's face]* Then why would you want to sing such a selfish song about hoarding up toys for yourself?

ZEKE: *[looks at toys in his hands]* Are you talking about these toys?

TUCKER: Yes, the very ones you're holding in your hands and singing so loudly about.

ZEKE: Well, these toys aren't for me, Tucker. Didn't you hear the minister tell about the new family in town? They have a boy named Brent who is about our age. Their house caught on fire last week and they lost everything. Brent lost all of his favorite toys. The minister asked us to pray about what we could give to help them this Christmas.

TUCKER: You mean you aren't singing selfishly about these toys? I know how much you wanted a toy helicopter and a new dump truck.

ZEKE: Nope, they aren't for me. I believe God wants me to help someone in need.

TUCKER: *[takes toys from Zeke]* And you are going to give these to Brent.

ZEKE: Yep, I was just on my way home now and my mom was going to help me wrap them and take me over to the motel where they are staying.

TUCKER: I just have one question. How did you get money to buy these toys? They are really nice.

ZEKE: I prayed and asked the Lord to help me find a way to help Brent.

TUCKER: And what happened?

ZEKE: Well, the phone rang and it was Mrs. Turner. Do you remember her?

TUCKER: Yes, isn't she taking care of her husband who got hurt?

ZEKE: Yep, that's her. Well, she asked my mom if it would be okay if I could come over and keep her husband company while she ran some errands.

Tucker: And she gave you some money to buy these toys?

Zeke: Well, not exactly. She bought me this helicopter to thank me for sitting with her husband.

Tucker: *[slaps Zeke's arm gently]* No kidding!

Zeke: I told her she didn't have to give me anything for visiting with her husband, but she insisted. I told her about Brent and his family. I asked her if I could give the helicopter to Brent. She said I could and then she brought out a new dump truck, and said she wanted Brent to have that too. Now can you see why I sing, "Toys to the world, the Lord has some?"

Tucker: Wow, Zeke! I sure do.

Zeke: I guess when you really think about it, Christmas is a time when the Lord wants to use us to bring His joy to the world. And a helicopter and dump truck sure will make one boy smile.

Tucker: You've got that right, Zeke. I'm going to pray about how Jesus can use me to bring His joy to the world too.

Zeke: *[looks troubled]* I can't figure out one thing though.

Tucker: What's that?

Zeke: I can't figure out who Harold is.

Tucker: Harold who?

Zeke: Harold the angel.

Tucker: What are you talking about?

Zeke: You know at church they are always singing about . . . *[sings]* Hark Harold the Angel Sings . . .

Tucker: *[pats Tucker's back and starts to walk off stage]* Let me try to explain it to you, Zeke. There's really not an angel named Harold. Technically the words are "Hark the herald angels sing."

Zeke: *[gasp]* But what happened to Harold?

Tucker: It's a long story, Zeke! It's a long story!

[dim lights and exit]

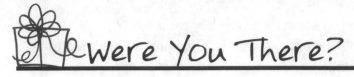
Were You There?

CAROL S. REDD

Summary: An attempt to interview some of those who were there when Jesus was born.

Characters:

INTERVIEWER

TWO STARS

INNKEEPER

THREE ANIMALS

ANGEL

JOSEPH

MARY

CHILD FROM AUDIENCE

Setting: church auditorium decorated for Christmas

Set: INTERVIEWER at front/center of stage. All other actors (other than CHILD FROM AUDIENCE) are spaced apart and standing in various places onstage. TWO STARS are standing together.

Props: hand-held microphone for INTERVIEWER

Costumes: appropriate costumes are needed for each actor with the exception of the INTERVIEWER and CHILD FROM AUDIENCE who are dressed in everyday casual clothes.

Running Time: 10-15 minutes

As drama begins, INTERVIEWER *addresses the audience.*

INTERVIEWER: It was a night like none other, for the world was about to change *forever!* Come back with me as we hear the sounds. There are muffled noises, babies crying, people talking, animals walking about, eating, and making various sounds and it's dark! Very, very dark . . . but look up at the stars! The bright twinkling stars . . . how many are there? Hundreds? Thousands? Millions? And take in the smells . . . the dustiness of the roads . . . the weary, sweaty animals . . . and the distant burning fires. But, wait . . . this isn't *my* story . . . so, perhaps it would be better if we talked to some who were actually there.

Interviewer walks over to the Two Stars.

INTERVIEWER: Pardon me, but I was hoping to find someone who might have been around when Jesus was born.

STAR #1: *[boastfully]* Well . . . that's me, so you've come to the right place. I was there all right . . . saw this young couple pull up in an SUV *[STAR #2 clears throat]*, uh, I mean a gold chariot . . . yeah, that's it, they were in a gold chariot *[STAR #2 clears throat]*. Well, maybe it wasn't *gold* exactly . . . maybe it was just an ordinary non-gold type chariot *[STAR #2 clears throat]*. Okay . . . okay . . . they weren't *in* anything! I think the lady was just sitting on an elephant *[STAR #2 clears throat]*. Okay! I mean a donkey . . . she was just sitting on a donkey and the man was walking along side her . . . carrying a lot of baby toys *[STAR #2 clears throat]*. No, I don't mean a *lot* of baby toys . . . just a few and he was pushing a baby stroller *[STAR #2 clears throat]*. Okay, okay, he wasn't carrying or pushing anything! *[shaking his head and rolling his eyes]* Are you happy now? *[STAR #2 nods and smiles as both stars exit.]*

INTERVIEWER: Well, let's see, maybe we can find someone else. Ah, here's someone. *[addressing INNKEEPER]* Pardon me sir, but I'm looking for someone who might have been around when Jesus was born.

INNKEEPER: Oh . . . here we go again! Yep, it's me . . . the Innkeeper! The one who told Mary and Joseph and their soon-to-be-born baby Jesus that I had no room for them in the inn. Good grief! I didn't know it was *the* Jesus! I just thought it was an ordinary couple, about to have an ordinary baby, who came in town for the census just like everyone else! Can you cut me some slack here? I mean it's been over 2,000 years and I'm still getting criticized for this one mistake! Like I said, I didn't realize it was *the* Jesus or I would have worked something out . . . might have even given them *my* bed if I had known . . . just give me a break! *[storms off-stage]*

INTERVIEWER: Okay then . . . let's see if we can find someone else . . . oh, look, here are some animals . . . maybe they were there. *[addressing animals]* Excuse me, but I was hoping to find someone who might have been present the night Jesus was born. *[All nod excitedly.]* Wonderful! Well, can you tell me exactly what happened that night? All the details . . . don't leave out a thing . . . I mean we are talking about Jesus, our Savior, so I want to know everything!

ANIMAL #1: Couldn't eat.

ANIMAL #2: A baby was in my straw.

ANIMAL #3: I was hungry . . . really, really hungry.

[All shake heads as they slowly exit stage.]

INTERVIEWER: Well, let's try again . . . surely there is someone who can provide us with a few more details. *[addressing angel]* Excuse me, but I was just trying to find someone who might have been around when Jesus was born.

ANGEL: I was there, and I'll never forget it!

INTERVIEWER: Oh, really? And why is that?

ANGEL: Because I got to sing with my other angel friends that night. You see, the night Jesus was born an angel appeared to some shepherds as they were watching their sheep. He told them that the Savior had been born in Bethlehem and that He was in a manger. That's when our angel choir burst out in song, "Glory to God in the highest, and on Earth peace toward men." Wow! That was just awesome! I'll never, ever forget it! *[exits as continues speaking]* Glory to God in the highest, and on Earth peace toward men. Whew! What a night!

INTERVIEWER: Okay, now I think we're starting to see just how exciting it was to be at the birth of Jesus. Oh, wait, let's check with this gentleman . . . he might know something. *[approaches Joseph]* Pardon me sir, but I was just trying to find someone who might have been around when Jesus was born.

JOSEPH: Well then, you've accomplished your mission. I was definitely there.

INTERVIEWER: Really? And what exactly were you doing?

Joseph: Well, I'm Joseph . . . you may have heard of me.

Interviewer: Joseph? Oh my, of course we've heard of you!

Joseph: Well, I was there *[thoughtfully]* . . . I can still remember how exhausted we were. Traveling so far . . . trying so hard to get a room because we knew it was almost time for the baby to be born. It was so frustrating and I was so very worried about Mary. But when it finally happened . . . when the baby was born . . . the baby we had been told to name "Jesus" . . . everything was perfect. Yes, it was simply a perfect night. *[exits]*

Interviewer: Wow . . . now I am starting to feel as though I was actually there. Jesus' birth . . . angels singing . . . Joseph's perfect night. *[sees Mary]* Oh wait, let's talk to this lady, maybe she knows something more. *[addressing Mary]* Excuse me, but I was hoping to find someone who might have been around when Jesus was born.

Mary: Well, I was certainly there . . . I am Mary . . . Jesus' mother.

Interviewer: Mary . . . wow! This is wonderful! You know absolutely everything about that glorious night! So what thoughts can you share with us?

Mary: Well, there are so many, many details . . . things that I hold so close to my heart . . . things that are almost too precious to put in to words. So let me just assure you that nothing . . . *nothing* . . . is impossible with God. *[exits]*

Interviewer: I am so overwhelmed by all of this . . . the stars, the innkeeper, the animals, Joseph, Mary . . . what more could we ask? *[slowly]* Well, actually, there is *one* more thing we could ask. If only Jesus Himself were here so we could talk to Him about His birth . . . how perfect would that be?

Child From Audience: *[walks up onstage]* Jesus *is* here, and we *can* talk to Him.

Interviewer: But . . .

Child From Audience: Really! We can. I do it every day. *[kneels down on stage, folds hands, and closes eyes]* Dear Jesus, thank You for being born in Bethlehem. Help us all to remember that You did that because You love us so much. We love You too. Merry Christmas, Jesus. Amen.

A Life Changing Experience

MARSHA R. CHUDY

Summary: The members of the youth group are asked to take part in the Living Nativity play. Much to their surprise, it turns out to be a life changing experience for them.

Characters: To simplify matters, the characters in Scene 1 are identified by the names of the biblical characters they portray in Scene 3.

HEROD—adult

MARY—preteen

JOSEPH—preteen

SHEPHERD—preteen

FIRST WISE MAN—preteen

ANGEL—preteen

SECOND WISE MAN—preteen

THIRD WISE MAN—preteen

ANGEL CHOIR—all ages

Setting: Scene 1—present day; a room in the church

Scene 2—biblical times

Scene 3—biblical times

Props: Scene 1—five chairs

Scene 3—Baby Jesus wrapped with strips of cloth

Costumes: Scene 1—All of the characters are dressed in modern-day casual clothes.

Scene 2—The ANGELS are dressed in white costumes and have gold halos.

Scene 3—All of the characters are dressed in Bible-times clothing. They all wear sandals. The WISE MEN have beards and expensive-looking clothes. HEROD also has expensive-looking clothes, and he is wearing a crown. The ANGEL is dressed in white and has a gold halo and wings.

Music: "Silent Night" and "Go Tell It on the Mountain"

Running Time: approximately 15-20 minutes

Scene 1

HEROD, MARY, JOSEPH, and SHEPHERD enter. HEROD remains standing and the other three sit on the chairs which are placed in a semi-circle.

HEROD: Is everyone here? *[looks around]* No? We'll wait a few more minutes.

MARY: What's so important that we had to come to a special meeting?

HEROD: I'll tell you when everyone gets here.

JOSEPH: I know. We're going to plan our Christmas party, right?

HEROD: Just wait. I want it to be a big surprise.

SHEPHERD: I don't think I like the sound of that.

JOSEPH: The last time someone told me it would be a big surprise, I spent the whole day cleaning out our garage.

[The WISE MEN and ANGEL enter and sit on the empty chairs and on the floor.]

HEROD: Is anyone else coming? *[He looks around as the others shake their heads.]* Let's get started. Christmas is only three weeks away, and the minister approached me the other day and asked—

JOSEPH: *[interrupts]* This can't be good.

HEROD: As I was saying, the minister would like to have the youth group help out with the Living Nativity play this year.

MARY: Why does he need us? The grownups always do it.

FIRST WISE MAN: Maybe he wants us to help set it up.

ANGEL: That shouldn't take too long.

SECOND WISE MAN: Count me in.

HEROD: Actually, that's not what he had in mind.

JOSEPH: I knew there was a catch.

MARY: Maybe he wants us to serve the hot chocolate and cookies.

HEROD: No, it's a little more than that.

MARY: We don't have to actually make the cookies do we? I refuse to be held responsible if anyone gets sick from eating mine.

SHEPHERD: Is Mrs. Foster going to make cookies? Hers are the best! I'll pass out her cookies.

FIRST WISE MAN: You just want to eat them.

SHEPHERD: Well, maybe just a couple.

HEROD: You're all wrong. He wants you to be in the play.

[There is total silence as they all look around at each other.]

HEROD: Don't all rush to volunteer.

THIRD WISE MAN: He wants us to do what?

ANGEL: I must not have heard you right. I thought you said that he wants us to actually be in the play.

HEROD: I did.

JOSEPH: You are kidding, aren't you?

ANGEL: So—what did you tell him?

HEROD: I said that I thought you would be glad to do it.

SHEPHERD: I think I'm going to be sick that day.

HEROD: But you don't even know when it is.

SECOND WISE MAN: That's okay. I'll manage to be sick no matter what day it is.

FIRST WISE MAN: I'm going to be busy then.

HEROD: Actually, that shouldn't be a problem. It's at the same time you normally come to our youth meeting, so you would be here anyway.

MARY: But Christmas plays are for little kids. People our age don't do that kind of thing. *[pauses]* At least, I don't.

SHEPHERD: Yeah, we really can't do something like that. What would our friends say?

ANGEL: They'll probably make fun of us.

HEROD: I guarantee, it will be a life changing experience.

FIRST WISE man: Yeah, our friends won't want to hang around with us anymore.

[The others nod in agreement.]

HEROD: Okay, quiet down now. We need to decide which part each of you will play.

JOSEPH: You can be Herod. He was mean, just like you. *[laughs]* Just kidding.

ANGEL: I want to be the angel. I never got to be one when I was little.

SHEPHERD: I don't want to be a smelly old shepherd.

FIRST WISE MAN: I want to wear a beard so my friends won't recognize me.

JOSEPH: I'm not going to do it if I have to wear a bathrobe.

MARY: What kind of costumes are there?

HEROD: They're in the other room. Let's go see what there is.

[They all exit.]

Scene 2

The ANGEL CHOIR enters and sings "Silent Night" and then exits.

Scene 3

MARY [carrying Baby Jesus], JOSEPH, and the SHEPHERD enter and stand together in a group toward one side. The WISE MEN and HEROD enter and stand together toward the other side. The ANGEL enters and stands toward the back, between the two groups. As the characters deliver their speeches, they turn and speak to the audience.

MARY: I wonder what it was like for Mary. She must have been afraid of what Joseph would say when he found out she was pregnant. I know it was an honor to be chosen by God to give birth to His Son, but it still would have been hard for her. I can't imagine having to travel so far in her condition. I got tired doing the three mile charity walk last year. I guess they didn't have cute baby clothes back then, because in the Bible it says that she wrapped Jesus in strips of cloth. *[pauses a moment and tucks cloths around baby]* I would feel horrible if I had to use pieces of cloth like this for my baby. It must have been scary having her baby in a stable. I wouldn't let all those dirty shepherds near my baby. She didn't seem to mind, though. I wonder if she let them touch Him. *[pauses]* I'm glad we did this this. Christmas seems more special to me this year. Usually, I forget about the meaning of Christmas because I get so busy thinking about parties and presents.

JOSEPH: Joseph must have been angry when he found out that Mary was pregnant. I know I would have been. I looked at a map, and it's over

sixty miles from Nazareth to Bethlehem. I'll bet Joseph's feet really
hurt by the time he got there. Mine do, and I've only been standing here
a little while. Back then they didn't have cool shoes like we do now.
They just wore sandals. It's too bad the innkeeper didn't have a room
for them. I wonder if Joseph felt bad because he wasn't able to provide
a nice place for the baby to be born. *[pauses]* Being in this Living
Nativity play isn't so bad after all. A lot of people have come to see us.

Shepherd: The shepherds were out in the fields watching over their sheep
the night Jesus was born. It says in the Bible that the shepherds were
terrified when a bright light appeared and an angel spoke to them. Then
a whole bunch of heavenly beings came and started singing. I would
have been scared too. The shepherds were so excited that they rushed

off to see the baby. Afterwards, they went around telling everyone about Jesus. It makes me think—when was the last time I was excited enough to tell people about Jesus?

HEROD: The Wise Men believed King Herod when he said that he wanted to worship the baby too. He sure fooled them. He wasn't interested in worshiping Jesus. Herod wanted to kill Jesus. I don't know how he could live with himself after ordering all those young boys to be killed. I'm sure Herod thought that he won, but in the end, he was the real loser.

FIRST WISE MAN: Traveling all the way from the East must have been brutal in those days. There weren't any cars, trains, or planes back then. It would have taken the Wise Men months to reach Bethlehem. They thought it was worth it, though, to see the king of the Jews. When I think of all they went through, I feel bad about complaining when I was asked to be in this play.

SECOND WISE MAN: The Wise Men probably expected to find Jesus in a palace. I'll bet they were shocked when they found out that He was born in a stable. They gave Him expensive gifts—gold, incense, and myrrh. Gifts fit for a king. I don't have much money. I wonder what I could give Jesus.

THIRD WISE MAN: It's a good thing the Wise Men were warned not to tell Herod where Jesus was. *[to the other Wise Men]* Look, there's Eric. He makes fun of me because I'm a Christian. He'll probably give me a hard time the next time he sees me. I don't care, though. I'm glad we did this play.

SECOND WISE MAN: I wonder if we could do it again next year. Maybe I could be the Shepherd.

ANGEL: *[steps forward]* You would have expected the angel to announce the birth of Jesus to the religious leaders, but he didn't. God sent the angel to humble shepherds. Jesus came to save everyone—the rich and the poor, the young and the old, people from every nation.

[ANGEL CHOIR enters singing the first verse of "Go Tell It on the Mountain."]

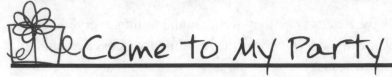

Come to My Party

IRIS GRAY DOWLING

Summary: MIKE, disappointed when no one came to his first party, prepared a new invitation to a Christmas/birthday party to tell why Jesus came from Heaven.

Characters:

MIKE—seven years old

JENNA—Mike's older sister

Setting: in MIKE's house

Props: stuffed animal

Running Time: 5 minutes

MIKE *holds his stuffed animal and looks sad.*

JENNA: What's wrong, Mike?

MIKE: *[sniffing]* I wanted to have a party.

JENNA: Why don't you?

MIKE: I don't have a reason. My birthday is too far away and I don't want to get laughed at.

JENNA: So a birthday party for you is not a good idea. How about a Christmas birthday party?

MIKE: What do you mean? My birthday isn't on Christmas.

JENNA: No, I mean celebrate Jesus' birthday.

MIKE: Oh, I never thought about His birthday being so close.

JENNA: You could invite your friends for games and stories. Then you can tell them about Jesus' birthday.

MIKE: *[says sadly]* I invited my friends to a party before, and no one came.

JENNA: No one?

MIKE: Just my little furry friend here. *[hugs bear]*

JENNA: You actually invited your friends . . . no fooling?

MIKE: Yep, some school friends.

JENNA: Did you send an invitation?

MIKE: *[says slowly]* No, I told them what day to come.

JENNA: Did you tell them what time?

MIKE: No, I forgot.

JENNA: Then how would their parents know anything about a party?

MIKE: I didn't think of that. I thought my friends would be glad to come, like yours do.

JENNA: Mine ask their parents first. What you need to do is start over. Make up some invitations. Be sure to put a date, time, place, and phone number on them.

MIKE: Okay.

JENNA: I'm sure your friends will come to a Christmas party for stories and games. Tell them not to bring gifts.

MIKE: Do you really think they'll come?

JENNA: At the party you could tell how Jesus came from Heaven to be born in Bethlehem. There are some places in the Bible where God said Jesus was coming to Earth.

MIKE: Where?

JENNA: Micah 5:2 says, "Bethlehem Ephratah, though you are small among the tribes of Judah, out of you will come for me one who will be ruler over Israel . . ."

MIKE: Is that all the Bible says about Jesus' birth?

JENNA: No. Isaiah 7:14 says, "Therefore the Lord himself will give you a sign: The virgin will be with child and will give birth to a son, and will call him Immanuel." And Matthew 1: 21 says, "She will give birth to a son, and you are to give him the name Jesus, because he will save his people from their sins."

MIKE: With all those announcements, weren't there lots of people anxious to be in Bethlehem to meet Jesus?

JENNA: I'm afraid not. Remember the innkeeper? He didn't know Mary was going to give birth to Jesus. He did not give them room to rest.

MIKE: How sad! There was no room for the baby from Heaven to be born.

JENNA: The innkeeper kept refusing a place to rest, but finally he let them go to the stable and that's where Jesus was born.

MIKE: Jesus had some animals in the stable just like I had my little bear at my first party.

JENNA: I didn't think about that, but God sent the angels from Heaven to announce Jesus' birth to some shepherds. As they sat out in the dark field with their animals they were frightened to see a bright light.

MIKE: Did they go to Bethlehem to see the Heavenly baby?

JENNA: Yes, they left their sheep and went quickly to find Jesus.

MIKE: I think I can find a picture of the shepherds kneeling to worship Jesus.

JENNA: When they left the stable they couldn't keep the news to themselves, so they told everyone they met about Jesus' birth.

MIKE: Wow! They were busy. What about the Wise Men?

JENNA: They followed the star to Bethlehem. They came so far that they didn't make it to the stable to worship Jesus.

MIKE: Where did they find Him?

JENNA: Because they arrived later, Mary and Joseph had moved to a house. They brought Jesus very special gifts.

MIKE: Did anyone tell them to do that?

JENNA: I think they were guided by God. There is nothing wrong with giving gifts, but people today sometimes think more about the gifts than about Jesus.

MIKE: What do you mean?

JENNA: The reason Jesus came to Earth was to bring us the gift of salvation.

MIKE: I know Jesus died on the cross for our sins.

JENNA: Yes, He took our punishment. He left this earth by inviting all people to accept His free gifts of forgiveness and salvation.

MIKE: Where does the Bible say that?

JENNA: John 14:6 says, "Jesus said, I am the way, the truth, and the life: no man comes to the Father except through me." Jesus meant we must accept Him as our Savior to get to Heaven.

MIKE: I have accepted His invitation to be my Savior.

JENNA: Then you have accepted another invitation. Those who accept Jesus as their Savior have also accepted the invitation to a banquet party in Heaven.

MIKE: Is everyone invited?

JENNA: Yes, but not all will be there.

MIKE: Why not?

JENNA: Some people ignore the invitation and some just refuse God's salvation gift.

MIKE: How can I help people not to ignore God's invitation?

JENNA: Have your party so you can tell this good news to your friends. Get your invitations ready. If you want me to look at them to see that you didn't leave anything out this time, let me know.

MIKE: All right. I'll go get started right now. *[exits right stage]*

JENNA: Okay, Mike. See you later. *[exits left stage]*

[This skit can be in introduction to invite kids to a Christmas birthday party for Jesus at which the children can have a time of fun, stories, games, and refreshments. A short devotional about Christmas can be given and Christmas story tracts included with some party favors to take home.]

Come to My Party

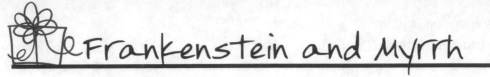

Frankenstein and Myrrh

JOHN COSPER

Characters:

MARY & JOSEPH—kids in costume

MIKE, HARRY, and DWAYNE—kids dressed like the wise men

MISS BAUER—a drama director

Two kids dressed as MARY and JOSEPH are on stage, kneeling beside a manger. MIKE, HARRY, and DWAYNE enter, dressed as the three kings. HARRY has a bottle hidden in his cloak. MIKE has a small bag. DWAYNE has a Frankenstein doll.

MIKE: Where is he who is born King of the Jews? We have seen his star in the East, and have come to worship him.

MARY: Here he is, lying in the manger.

MIKE: Look! It's the Christ child, just as the prophecy told us.

HARRY: What is his name?

MARY: His name is Jesus.

MIKE: We worship you, Jesus. We come bearing gifts of gold.

[MIKE sets down his bag before the manger.]

HARRY: And myrrh.

[HARRY sets his bottle down.]

DWAYNE: And Frankenstein!

[Dwayne pulls out the Frankenstein doll.]

JOSEPH: Frankenstein? That's not in the script!

DWAYNE: Yes it is!

MARY: Miss Bauer! Dwayne's messing up the play.

[Miss Bauer enters. Dwayne grabs the Frankenstein doll.]

BAUER: What's the matter?

MARY: Will you tell Dwayne there's no Frankenstein in the Christmas story?

DWAYNE: There is too! It's in the Bible!

MIKE: It's not Frankenstein. It's frankincense.

DWAYNE: Frankincense? What's that?

BAUER: It's a spice, Dwayne.

DWAYNE: A spice? You mean like salt and pepper?

BAUER: Something like that.

DWAYNE: A baby's not gonna want that! It'll burn His tongue! Babies need toys. That's why I brought Him Frankenstein.

BAUER: The wise men didn't give Jesus a Frankenstein doll.

DWAYNE: You mean they gave Him the movie? How would He watch it?

HARRY: Oh, I can't work like this! I'll be in my trailer.

[HARRY storms off.]

MIKE: I think he means the bathroom.

BAUER: Thank you, Mike. Why don't you run along after him?

MARY: Are we on a break?

BAUER: Yes, we are.

[MARY, JOSEPH, and MIKE exit. Dwayne starts to go, but Miss Bauer grabs his elbow.]

BAUER: Not so fast, Dwayne.

DWAYNE: I'm not in trouble, am I?

BAUER: No. I just wanted to make sure you understood what your gift meant.

Dwayne: I know what it means. He's a boy. He wants toys, and boys like scary toys.

Bauer: Dwayne, Frankenstein wasn't written until over 1800 years after Jesus was born. There was no Frankenstein. But there was frankincense.

Dwayne: Why would a baby want cooking spices?

Bauer: Frankincense isn't for cooking, Dwayne. Frankincense was a very valuable spice, usually reserved for kings and queens. In fact, all of Jesus' gifts were gifts fit for a king.

Dwayne: I know kings liked gold a lot. But what about the myrrh and frankincense?

Bauer: Those were both valuable spices, like I said. Both of those gifts were probably worth more than the gold!

Dwayne: Whoa! What did they use it for?

Bauer: It was used for funerals.

Dwayne: Funerals!

Bauer: That's right. When a person died, they would wrap the body in linen. But only the wealthiest people were able to add spices like myrrh and frankincense.

Dwayne: But why would they give funeral spices to a baby?

Bauer: Because Jesus was born for one purpose: to save us from our sins. And in order to do that, He had to die on the cross.

Dwayne: That's so sad!

Bauer: Dwayne, you know Jesus rose from the dead. And in doing so, He gave all of us the chance to have eternal life. That's why we celebrate Christmas.

Dwayne: I guess you're right. But I still think those wise men should have brought Jesus a toy.

Bauer: I'm sure baby Jesus had plenty of toys, just like any ordinary baby.

Dwayne: But He wasn't an ordinary baby, was He?

Bauer: No, Dwayne, He certainly was not.

The Toys Nobody Wants

JOHN COSPER

Characters:
THE PINK RAVER
GI JACK
DRAGON SMASHER
THE REVEREND D.L. MOODY

The Pink Blazer is on stage alone.

PINK: Hey! Hey you, looking for that last minute gift? Come on, I'm right here! I know your kid watches the show. I know he's got the rest of my team. Why not complete it with the Pink Raver! *[does a karate kick]* See that? That's right, I got mad skills! Hey! No need to ask that salesperson for help. I'm right here! Just take me home, wrap me up . . . No! Not another one! Come on, dude! It's Christmas Eve! I don't wanna be here alone!

[GI JACK enters.]

JACK: Sad, isn't it?
PINK: Me or them?
JACK: Being overlooked.
PINK: What do you mean, overlooked? I'm one of the stars of the top-rated after school show for boys 8-12.
JACK: Key word: boys. Boys want to play with action figures. Not dolls.
PINK: What are you talking about? I am an action figure!
JACK: You have a skirt. That's why you're still here five minutes 'til closing on Christmas Eve, and all your compatriots are wrapped up under trees all over town.
PINK: Hey, I wouldn't talk, pal. I'm not the only one in danger of spending Christmas on the shelf!

Jack: Oh, I got over that a long time ago. Matter of fact, this is my third Christmas here.

Pink: Who are you?

Jack: GI Jack.

Pink: Any relation to—

Jack: None at all. I'm half the price, and twice the fun—so says my box. But as you can probably guess, without the brand name, I'm pretty much going nowhere.

Pink: I guess not.

[Dragon Smasher enters.]

Dragon: Hey! Is that guy still here? I don't think he saw me!

Jack: Don't kid yourself, pal. There's a whole end cap of you. If he wanted you, he'd have you.

Dragon: Put a cork in it, Generic Joe! I'm not some two-bit knock off of a real toy. I'm the lead character in the summer's biggest blockbuster!

Jack: Didn't you close after two weeks?

Pink: Who is this guy?

Dragon: Dragon Smasher, the biggest blockbuster movie ever to come out of Hollywood! Three hundred million dollar budget, shot on four continents.

Jack: Came in fifth place opening weekend.

Dragon: You just wait 'til we hit the video market.

Jack: You did. Your movie's in the $3.99 bin up front with *Problem Child 4.*

Pink: Great. I'm stuck here on Christmas with two losers!

Dragon: Hey, do you know who almost played me in the movie? If it wasn't for that stupid flu—

[D.L. Moody enters. He is in a suit and has a CLEARANCE sign on the front.]

Moody: Merry Christmas, brothers and sisters. The peace of Christ be with you all.

The Toys Nobody Wants

DRAGON: Who is this guy?

MOODY: The name's Moody. D.L. Moody, world-renowned evangelist.

PINK: An evangelist action figure?

MOODY: From the Heroes of the Faith Action Figure and Toy Line. We, uh, we weren't exactly a hit, as you can see.

JACK: I guess not.

DRAGON: Wow, I guess they'll make an action figure out of anybody.

JACK: They made you, didn't they?

DRAGON: Hey, I'm not the guy with the Clearance sticker!

[Jack rips a Clearance sticker off DRAGON SMASHER's back and hands it to him.]

DRAGON: Aw, man!

PINK: Great. I could be in some kid's home, playing with my pals and flying in my Iguana-Zord. Instead, I'm stuck here with Commando Rip-Off, a box office flop, and a preacher.

MOODY: Take heart, pink space warrior. You're not the first to spend Christmas without a home. Why on the very first Christmas of all, Jesus Christ slept in a food trough for animals, without a roof over His head.

PINK: He did?

MOODY: Oh yes, the King of kings was turned away from the inn. But that's how He planned it. He wanted it known, from the beginning, that He was not here for those who have it all. He came for those who have nothing, the misfits, the outcasts.

PINK: He did?

MOODY: Oh yes. It's sad how people lose sight of the Christ child at this time of year. People are so consumed with finding the right gifts and having the perfect holiday dinner, they forget why we came to celebrate Christmas in the first place.

JACK: Commerce?

MOODY: No, GI Jack. Christmas is the fulfillment of a promise that God would save His children from their sins. And not just those who were wealthy and powerful. Anyone can receive the gift of salvation, no matter who they are, how rich or poor they are, or what they have done. Yes, friends, Jesus came to save the friendless, the lonely, the outcast.

DRAGON: *[almost in tears]* You mean, Jesus came for people . . . like me?

MOODY: Sorry, Dragon Smasher, we're just a bunch of toys. Jesus did not die for us.

DRAGON: Aww.

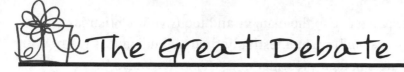

The Great Debate

DIANNE MCINTOSH

Summary: Two teams debate the real reason for Christmas.

Characters:

MODERATOR—host of the debate

SS 1—arrogant and opinionated spokesperson for SANTA SAINTS debate team

SS 2—arrogant and opinionated spokesperson for SANTA SAINTS debate team

AUDIENCE 1 thru 6—members of the enthusiastic studio audience. The audience can be as large or small as needed.

MM 1—sincere spokesperson for MOVE TO THE MANGER debate team

MM 2—sincere spokesperson for MOVE TO THE MANGER debate team

Setting: a stage with two debate teams.

Props: computer mouse, giant Christmas stocking, fluffy pillow, toy, face cream, CPAP machine, Santa hat, cell phone, doll, bun, camera, computer game, small plastic Santa with reindeer, manger

Running Time: 20 Minutes

SANTA SAINTS and MOVE TO THE MANGER debate teams are seated at two different tables, stage left, with papers in front of them. Their scripts can be on these papers. The MODERATOR is seated center stage behind a small podium. The AUDIENCE is seated stage right.

MODERATOR: *[reading from "notes"]* Christmas. What is it? What elements are culturally relevant and what parts of celebrating the season are outdated and old fashioned? Here tonight to answer these questions are two dynamic teams of debaters. On my left is the Santa Saints Team. The S.S. groupies are dedicated to celebrating the season with all the flash and dash of Santa's reindeer plus they're open minded enough to add any other element that promotes festive fun. On my right is the Move to the Manger Team. These loyal traditionalists believe the birth of Jesus is the reason for the entire holiday season. Who is right? Will you join Santa's saints in an anything-goes holiday smorgasbord?

Or will you take a move to the manger and focus your Christmas celebration on Jesus? Tonight a festively fired-up audience is ready to assist our debaters in their presentations [AUDIENCE *cheers*].

MODERATOR: First question: Why do we celebrate Christmas?

Ss1: We'd like to present our case by asking the audience why *they* celebrate Christmas.

MODERATOR: Fair enough. Audience, why do you celebrate Christmas?

AUDIENCE 1: To get lots of new toys!

AUDIENCE 2: I love the yummy food.

AUDIENCE 3: Because we get two weeks off from school.

AUDIENCE 4: I love Christmas movies.

AUDIENCE 5: Because it's fun!

AUDIENCE 6: I celebrate the birth of Jesus. I believe—

Ss2: [*interrupts*] Yes, yes. As you can see fun, movies, and toys are the reason *most* people celebrate the season. If you turn Christmas into a narrow minded, religious holiday you take the joy right out of the season.

Ss1: Exactly. Keep it open. Focus on fun! Make sure everyone gets what they want.

MODERATOR: Move to the Manger, what do you have to say to that?

Mm1: There isn't anything wrong with fun, but *fun* isn't the heart of Christmas. Audience, do any of the reasons why you celebrate Christmas last past the holidays?

AUDIENCE 1: Toys last. Well, they last for a while, unless my mom and dad get me some cheap thing that breaks the first time I play with it. If they'd spend some real money on me, *then* the toys would last.

AUDIENCE 2: My mom thinks the food lasts all year; at least she's always complaining about how she gains ten pounds at Christmas and has to work the whole rest of the year to get rid of it.

AUDIENCE 3: Well . . . the truth is . . . I get a little bored with two weeks off from school. I mean it's fun for a while but then I end up having to do a bunch of chores.

AUDIENCE 4: Movies don't actually last but they're fun while you're watching them. It's two hours of joy, which is better than nothing.

AUDIENCE 5: [*looks a little sad*] Every Christmas, right after I open all my presents, I feel a little let down, like now it's over and the fun's over too. I hate those after-Christmas blues.

Audience 6: *[brightly]* Jesus lasts all year.

Mm2: That's right! Jesus lasts all year. When you move to the manger and focus the Christmas celebration on Jesus you open a gift that never breaks, it gives joy for a lifetime, it isn't boring, and it never leaves you with the blues.

Ss1: But is it now, is it happening? If I remember right, Jesus was born 2,000 years ago. Why would anyone want to celebrate a baby in a manger when there are so many really cool, modern ways to have a holly, jolly Christmas?

Mm1: Don't you think it's amazing that after 2,000 years people still *are* celebrating the birth of Jesus?

Ss2: Some people don't know when to quit. Change is where it's at. The world is moving and changing so fast you have to step out of the stable and get on the *now*.

Mm2: Are you saying Santa Claus is now?

Ss1: *He* changes his message to fit what's happening in the world.

Moderator: *[clears throat]* Let's get back to *my* questions. How does music reflect and communicate the message of Christmas?

Ss1: That *is* an interesting question. I'm sure you're all aware of the impact music has on culture. Let's see . . . could the audience please help us with a few numbers? How about *Rudolph the Red Nosed Reindeer?*

[Audience sings part of Rudolph the Red Nosed Reindeer.]

Ss1: There, you see? What a wonderful example of Christmas. It's a modern success story, the kind of thing that everyone can embrace. Poor Rudolph is rejected because of a deformed nose but it turns out his personal problem is actually a gift and he's able to overcome the odds and become Santa's biggest helper.

Ss2: That story alone is an inspiration. What makes these songs so important is they're modern and culturally relevant. Santa is now. He's what people are looking for. *[snaps fingers]* Best example is the classic

Santa Claus is Coming to Town. Sing it audience.

[AUDIENCE sings "Santa Claus is Coming to Town."]

Ss2: That tells it all. Santa comes once a year and doles out the goods. And the truth is he doesn't keep *that* accurate of records on the good and bad kids. There's a curve based on who your parents are, where you live, who your teachers at school are, and whether you have high levels of stress in your life. Pretty much everyone turns out to be good.

Ss1: And that's what people really want, isn't it? They want to be told they're good.

Ss2: Plus the music is new, fresh, happening. It isn't some old, moldy song that's been sung for a couple hundred years. Santa songs tell it like it is.

Ss1: *[holds up finger, pointing]* . . . or at least how people want to hear it. And that's what Christmas is all about, getting what you want.

[AUDIENCE claps and cheers.]

MODERATOR: I think you've made some interesting points. Now it's time to hear what the Move to the Manger group has to say.

Mm1: Thank you. First of all, Santa isn't real. *[gasp from AUDIENCE and Ss TEAM]* The modern day Santa is a figment of someone's imagination. All the songs about him are simply made-up out of thin air. Jesus is real. He was really born and He really came to be our Savior. The songs about Him are all based on a real happening, a world changing, life transforming event. Let's take *Joy to the World* for instance. Audience, could you sing the first verse please?

[AUDIENCE sings first verse of "Joy to the World."]

Mm 2: The song *is* old but the message is *never* old. "Let every heart prepare him room," that's new to each person who accepts Jesus as Lord of their life. It's a gift that is personal to every person who makes a move to the manger.

Mm 1: Plus it doesn't require being good. It's a gift based on the grace of God. According to Santa's Saints, the standard for getting a gift from Santa is based on behavior. God's gift is based on love.

Moderator: Very interesting. You're saying that Jesus is a good gift for *this* generation even though He was born more than 2,000 years ago?

Mm 2: Yes. God is *now*. Nothing we create is new to God. Computers, the Internet . . . you name it and God is bigger than all of it. Moving to the manger opens the gift of God's love. It's the newest, freshest, and most culturally relevant gift anyone will ever receive.

Moderator: Let's move on. One of the most important elements of Christmas is stories. Stories capture our imagination. With this in mind Santa's Saints, would you share the story of Christmas from your perspective?

Ss1: We'll need audience participation for this one. The nature of the holiday changes and new celebrations emerge as people expand their thinking, but we've decided to take you back to the real heart of the Santa story because it says a lot.

Ss2: Yes, it says a lot. We've taken some liberties with the original St. Nicolas poem by Clement Clarke Moore. The transformation of the poem into modern lingo is just another way to illustrate the powerful message of Santa Claus. I'll read the poem. Audience, here is a box with items you will need to hold up as I read.

[Ss2 hands the Audience the box. Audience holds up items as Ss2 reads.]

It was the night before Christmas,
and all through the house
nothing was moving not even a mouse. *[hold up computer mouse]*
The biggie sized stockings *[giant stocking]*
were hung up with care
all because Santa Claus soon would be there.

The kids were all sleeping in large comfy beds *[put head on over-stuffed pillow]*
while visions of Transformers danced through their heads *[hold toy above*

head of sleeping child]
and Mom in her face cream and I in my CPAP *[jar of face cream,*
   breathing machine]
had just gone to sleep for a long winter's nap.
Then out in the front yard arose a loud clatter *[shake noise maker]*
I jumped out of bed to see what was the matter.
What do you think was out on the lawn?
A burglar? A stray dog? A giant Cybertron? *[stuffed dog]*
I blinked and I wondered then what did appear?
Santa's red sleigh and eight flying reindeer. *[Santa with red hat on]*
Wow, what a sight! It did give me pause
Yes it's true, I was seeing good old Santa Claus!

He came down our chimney and filled all the stockings
He gave Mom a new printer with camera docking *[small camera printer]*
He gave Jill a cell phone that connects to the net *[cell phone]*
Plus a Hannah Montana doll, the best you can get. *[doll]*
Santa Claus knew just what to give me
The latest techno game to set my mind free. *[computer type game]*
He didn't say a thing, he had work to get done
He doled out the goods then nibbled a bun. *[nibble bun]*
And laying a finger on the jet pack he wore,
He pressed a red button and up the chimney he soared.
He jumped in his sleigh and started to whistle
And away they all flew like a fast moving missile *[small rubber Santa*
   with sleigh thrown across the stage]
I saw his thumbs moving as he drove out of sight
"Merry Christmas to all and to all a good night"
was the message he texted to my waiting cell phone.
He waved one last time and then he was gone.

Ss1: *[smug]* You see Santa changes with the times. He isn't offering the
   same present this year that he doled out 2,000 years ago. Santa, and all
   the fun that goes with him, is the heart of Christmas. We rest our case.
Moderator: That was really great. Thank you. Now Move to the Manger,

are you ready with your presentation?

MM1: Yes. I'll read from the Bible, Luke 2:1-20. Here is the manger. *[MM2 puts the manger center stage.]* Audience I'd like you to move to the manger as the story is read.

[AUDIENCE members are each character of the story. As the story is read they place themselves around the manger. The nativity scene remains in place for the rest of the debate.]

MM2: Jesus gave people a lasting gift—a gift that never wears out, always fits, and never needs to be exchanged.

MM1: John 3:16 says, "For God so loved the world that he gave his one and only Son, that whoever believes in him shall not perish but have eternal life."

MM2: That verse says it all. God loves us and He is offering us a gift: eternal life. Jesus was born, the baby in the manger. We are loved by God. That's the real gift.

MM1: The gift never goes out of style. It's always culturally relevant. It's the reason to celebrate Christmas. Why don't all of you make a move to the manger and you'll see and know for yourself the love of God in your life. That's Christmas.

[The MOVE TO THE MANGER group looks at SANTA'S SAINTS and motions them to the manger.]

Ss1: You want us to move to the manger? Us? Santa's Saints?

Ss2: I am a little curious about that baby. Should we make a move to the manger? I mean, won't it ruin our whole Christmas?

MM2: It won't ruin it at all. Make a move to the manger. Come on, stand with us and accept Jesus' gift. Christmas will never be the same for you again.

[The MODERATOR, Ss1, Ss2, MM1, MM2 move around the manger and sing Joy to the World.]

The Star
Lenora McWhorter

NARRATOR: A light came from Heaven in the form of a star and lighted the way for the wise men to travel the distance to find the baby Jesus. The five-pointed star has special meaning about what Jesus' coming means to us.

CHILD # 1: *[hold up a star]* The first point on the star says, "God has come near." He is no longer a distant God in Spirit form. God had become flesh and lives with us.

CHILD # 2: *[hold up a star]* The second point of the star says, "Christ has come to show God's love for us." God had a plan that would free us from our sin. Jesus came to die for us.

CHILD # 3: *[hold up a star]* The third point on the star says, "God shows mercy to the lost." Because of God's love, He would give people a chance to turn from their sins and start a new life.

CHILD # 4: *[hold up a star]* The fourth point of the star says, "God will make known His kingdom to the world through His Son Jesus, as He bears witness to His followers."

CHILD # 5: *[hold up a star]* The fifth point of the star says, "God will send the Holy Spirit to live within us so we can be a witness to God's Word." The Holy Spirit would make God's presence felt on the earth.

NARRATOR: May the star shine bright this Christmas and all year to light the way for the lost to find their way to Jesus.

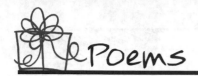 # Poems

The Innkeeper
Alan Cliburn

I am the innkeeper
and my inn could hold no more.
The "no vacancy" sign was hung
   out front,
yet someone's knocking at the
   door.

Opening the door just a crack,
"Can't you read the sign?" I said.
"Sir, the Baby's almost here,
all we need is a bed."

One look at the girl
told me it was true.
But every single room was full.
What could I possibly do?

They looked so tired standing
   there,
their donkey was nearby.
Suddenly an idea came to me;
it was certainly worth a try.

"There's a stable behind the inn,"
I heard myself say.
"It's not much, but warm and dry,
you can make a bed in the hay."

"Oh, thank you, sir, so very
   much,"
they said with tears in eye.
Then off they went and I headed
   for bed,
but why did I want to cry?

During the night I had a dream,
I could hear angels singing.
"Glory to God in the highest!"
Their voices, like bells, were
   ringing.

But was it only a dream?

I Wish
Alan Cliburn

I wish I was a shepherd boy
the night the angel came.
He proclaimed the birth of Christ
and nothing was ever the same.

I wish I was a stable boy
in that cave behind the inn.
Oh, if I could've seen the infant King,
who would save us from our sin.

If there were junior wise men
I'd sign up right away.
But when we found where Jesus was
I'd probably wish to stay!

I have one more wish to make,
a really important one too.
I wish you'd ask Jesus in your heart.
That's my special wish for you.

Merry Christmas!

Two Special Days
Alan Cliburn

Lights are twinkling everywhere,
but they don't tell the story.
Even plastic manger scenes
don't give Him His full glory.

The reason for the season
can't be found in any *thing*.
Christmas is found when we celebrate
the birth of Christ the King.

But He didn't stay a baby.
He grew up to be a man
who gave His life for you and me,
oh, what a wonderful plan!

Christmas and then Easter,
two very special days.
We need them both to be complete,
and He deserves our praise.

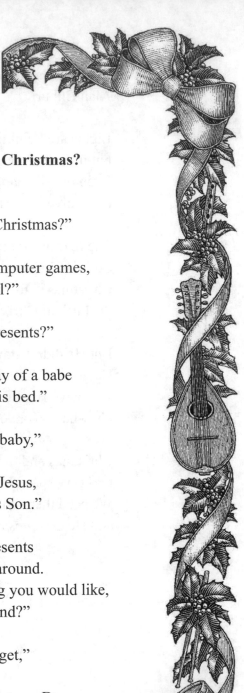

What Do You Want for Christmas?
Alan Cliburn

"What do you want for Christmas?"
they asked the little girl.
"A doll, some skates, computer games,
a baton that you can twirl?"

"But why should I get presents?"
the little girl said.
"Christmas is the birthday of a babe
who had a manger for His bed."

"But He wasn't just any baby,"
the little girl went on.
"They named the Baby Jesus,
and He was called God's Son."

"But everyone wants presents
when Christmas comes around.
There must be something you would like,
maybe candy by the pound?"

"No, I want to give, not get,"
the little girl told them.
"And on this happy Christmas Day,
I give myself to Him."

Little Baby Jesus
Crystal Bowman

Little baby Jesus,
do You know it's Christmas night?
Can You hear the angels singing?
Can You see the stars so bright?

Little baby Jesus,
do You know that long ago
the prophets said that You would come
to live on Earth below?

Little baby Jesus,
do You know you are the One
who will save the world from sin?
Do You know You are God's Son?

Little baby Jesus,
do You know that You will be
a teacher and a healer
who will help the blind to see?

Little baby Jesus,
do You know that You will die
and You'll hang upon a cross
as people watch and cry?

Little baby Jesus,
do You know that You will rise
and You'll leave the earth below
as You rise into the skies?

Little baby Jesus
I am glad that someday too,
I will live in Heaven
if I put my trust in You.

Come to the Town of Bethlehem
Crystal Bowman

Come to the town of Bethlehem;
the stars are shining so bright.
The angels are singing a chorus;
the Christ-child's been born tonight!

Come to the town of Bethlehem;
the shepherds have found Him
    asleep.
His bed is a wooden manger,
next to the donkeys and sheep.

Come to the town of Bethlehem,
then you will see Jesus too.
He is our Lord and Savior,
who was born for me and you.

God sent His Son to Bethlehem.
He came from heaven above.
He came to Earth to save us all
and show us God's great love.

Come to the town of Bethlehem
and worship the newborn King.
Jesus our Lord has come to Earth.
He is the reason we sing.

Holding Christmas
Karen M. Leet

[Instructions: Each child holds an object or picture of object while saying lines.]

I'm holding the star that shone in the sky
on Christmas Day, on Christmas Day.
I'm holding a sheep that stood in a field
on Christmas Day, on Christmas Day.
I'm holding a shepherd who guarded the sheep
on Christmas Day, on Christmas Day.
I'm holding an angel who sang the good news
on Christmas Day, on Christmas Day.
I'm holding the straw where Jesus lay
on Christmas Day, on Christmas Day.
I'm holding the cow that rested nearby
on Christmas Day, on Christmas Day.
I'm holding the Baby born today
on Christmas Day, on Christmas Day.

[All say] Baby Jesus, born this day,
on Christmas Day, on Christmas Day! Hooray, hooray!

Joy, Joy, Joy
Karen M. Leet

Joy, joy, joy I sing.
Christmas joy to you I bring.
Joy, joy, joy I'm singing.
Christmas joy Jesus is bringing.
Joy, joy, joy is my song.
I sing of Christmas all day long.

When I Think of Christmas
Dolores Steger

[a recitation for 3 or 6 speakers]

SPEAKER 1: When I think of Christmas, I think of a tree with gifts set beneath it, wrapped so carefully.

SPEAKER 2: When I think of Christmas, of St. Nick I think. His "Ho-ho," his presents, his nod and his wink.

SPEAKER 3: When I think of Christmas, it seems that I find all sorts of parties pop into my mind.

ALL: But wait!

SPEAKER 1 or 4: When I think of Christmas, I think of a star, followed by Wise Men who come from afar.

SPEAKER 2 or 5: When I think of Christmas, it's angels I see, and shepherds all worshiping on bended knee.

SPEAKER 3 or 6: When I think of Christmas, I see Bethlehem town, a manger, a Christ Child, the Son God sent down.

ALL: When we think of Christmas, one thing we must say to Jesus, our Savior, "Happy Birthday this day."

Noel, Noel
Dolores Steger

Noel, Noel, the angels tell
Christ's born on Christmas day.
Noel, Noel, the shepherds tell
in a manger bed He lay.
Noel, Noel, the Magi tell
the King of kings is He.
Noel, Noel the heavens tell
in Him people are free.

Looking at Jesus
Dolores Steger

I'm looking at Jesus,
so peaceful He lies,
under the bright stars
of Bethlehem skies.
Shepherds and Wise Men
are looking on too,
in awe at the wonder
of God's gift so new.
With Mary and Joseph,
and angels above,
we all look at Jesus;
we all see there Love.

Is It Time?
Dolores Steger

Is it time? I just can't wait
for that blest December date,
with gifts of love, I won't be late,
when Jesus' birth we celebrate.

A Farewell
Dolores Steger

Our program is ending,
so too is the year.
We wish you all happiness,
blessings, and cheer.
May sweet joy surround you
and those you hold dear.
May the Spirit of Christmas
forever be near.

Wonder of Wonders
Dolores Steger

Wonderful, wonderful, angels sing clear.
Wonderful, wonderful, shepherds draw near.
Wonderful wonderful, Wise Men appear.
Wonder of wonders, Lord Jesus is here!

Instructions to the Shepherds
Amy Houts

"Do not be afraid,"
said an angel from above.
"I bring you good news
of God's great love!"

"A baby is born!"
The trumpet sounded loud.
"Go and tell the news
Go and tell the crowd!"

The Eve of Christmas
Amy Houts

Colored lights and hopeful feelings
of the day to come.
Mistletoe hangs from the ceiling.
Decorating's done.

Church bells ringing to remind us
time to go to town.
Church pews fill with wet coats and scarves,
snow melts all around.

Sounds of sleigh bells, Christmas carols
ringing in my ears.
Midnight service, prayerful worship,
Christmas Day is here!

Happy Birthday, Jesus!
Amy Houts

Happy birthday, little One.
Happy birthday, God's own Son.
How many candles on Your cake?
How shall we start to celebrate?
What games do You want to play?
What decorations to display?
But more importantly,
what gift do You want from me?

All the People of the World
Amy Houts

Did you ever wonder why
the angels told the shepherds first,
and not the king or governor,
the miracle of our Savior's birth?

Shepherds humble, poor, and lowly,
showed God welcomes everyone,
all the people of the world,
to worship Jesus, God's own Son!

The Perfect Gift
Rebecca Haynes Mott

'Tis the season of giving, hold out your hands!
Here's a gift that's wonderful and full of God's plans.
God knows all about you, what you want and what you need.
And His gift will last forever, it needs no batteries!
Now it may seem impossible, too good to be true.
But He's sent it special delivery, from afar, just for you.
Open your hands, open your eyes . . . the perfect gift is come!
It's Jesus Christ, your Savior, God's one and only Son.

The Best Gift
Pamela Kessler

God sent a gift for Christmas,
so very long ago.
The gift was wrapped in swaddling cloths,
a halo was its bow.

This gift of life, a baby boy,
was sent in peace for all.
To show how much God loves us,
and to save us from the fall.

For we were lost deep in sin
and could not make it right.
So God sent His only Son
to save us from our plight.

Jesus is that perfect gift;
His life put sin to rest.
Though we deserve no gift at all,
God gave the very best.

Precious Gift
Amy Houts

"Glory to God and peace on Earth!"
The angels sang of the savior's birth.
We celebrate with family
this gift from God, to you and me.

So when you're passing gifts around,
hear Christmas carols lovely sound,
remember the most precious one,
a babe in the manger, God's own Son.